www.booksbyboxer.com

Published in the UK by
Books By Boxer, Leeds, LS13 4BS
© Books By Boxer 2016
All Rights Reserved

ISBN: 9781909732506

The exact origin of the Knock Knock joke is a little unclear, but many scholars consider Shakespeare's Macbeth to be the earliest known example. In act 2, scene 3, it occurs when a porter is awakened from a drunken stupor by a man knocking at Macbeth and Lady Macbeth's door.

The Knock Knock jokes first published appearance in popular culture is largely credited to a newspaper columnist in 1934. The joke was:

Knock Knock.
Who's there?
Rufus.
Rufus who?
Rufus the most important part of your house.

Despite this less than salubrious start, the Knock Knock joke has become engrained in our lives and regardless of how unfunny it is, never fails to raise a giggle!

Knock Knock.
Who's there?
Canoe
Canoe who?
Canoe come out and play?

Knock Knock.
Who's there?
Who
Who who?
That's what an
owl says!

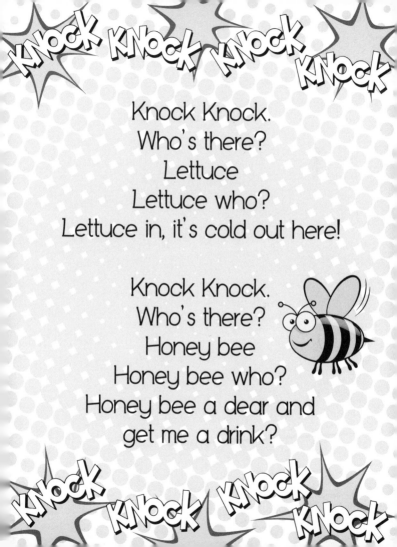

Knock Knock.
Who's there?
Lettuce
Lettuce who?
Lettuce in, it's cold out here!

Knock Knock.
Who's there?
Honey bee
Honey bee who?
Honey bee a dear and
get me a drink?

Knock Knock.
Who's there?
Wooden Shoe
Wooden shoe who?
Wooden shoe like to know!

Knock Knock.
Who's there?
Cow says
Cow says who?
No silly! Cows say moo!

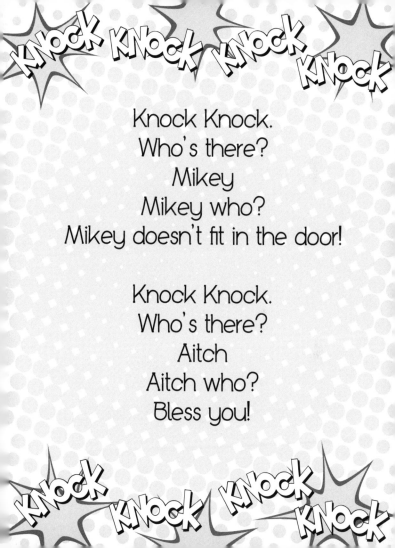

Knock Knock.
Who's there?
Mikey
Mikey who?
Mikey doesn't fit in the door!

Knock Knock.
Who's there?
Aitch
Aitch who?
Bless you!

Knock Knock.
Who's there?
I am
I am who?
You don't know who you are?

Knock Knock.
Who's there?
Ya
Ya who?
Wow! I'm excited to
see you too!

Knock Knock.
Who's there?
Figs
Figs who?
Figs the doorbell, it's broken

Knock Knock.
Who's there?
Boo
Boo who?
Don't cry, it's only me!

Knock Knock.
Who's there?
Interrupting pirate
Interrupting Pir...
AAARRRRR!!!
(You interrupt them)

Knock Knock.
Who's there?
Iva
Iva who?
Iva sore hand from knocking!

Knock Knock.
Who's there?
Butter
Butter who?
Butter not tell you,
you might not let me in!

Knock Knock.
Who's there?
A little old lady
A little old lady who?
I didn't know you could yodel!

Knock Knock.
Who's there?
Barbie
Barbie who?
BBQ chicken

Knock Knock.
Who's there?
Howard
Howard who?
Howard I know?

Knock Knock.
Who's there?
Dishes
Dishes who?
Dishes a very bad joke

Knock Knock.
Who's there?
Pencil
Pencil who?
Pencil fall down if
you don't wear a belt!

Knock Knock.
Who's there?
Smell mop
Smell mop who?
Eeeeww! I don't want
to smell your poo!

Knock Knock.
Who's there?
Cargo
Cargo who?
No... car go beep! beep!

Knock Knock.
Who's there?
Aaron
Aaron who?
Aaron you going to let me in?

Knock Knock.
Who's there?
Phillip
Phillip who?
Phillip my cup, I'm thirsty!

Knock Knock.
Who's there?
Doris
Doris who?
Dorrs locked! That's
why I'm knocking!

Knock Knock.
Come in!

Knock Knock.
Who's there?
Tickle
Tickle who?
Tickle YOU! (Tickle them as you say it)

Knock Knock.
Who's there?
Arthur
Arthur who?
Arthur any nice things
to eat in there?

Knock Knock.
Who's there?
Dwayne
Dwayne who?
Dwayne the bath quick!
I'm dwoning!

Knock Knock.
Who's there?
Spell
Spell who?
W-H-O

Knock Knock.
Who's there?
Ice cream soda
Ice cream soda who?
Ice cream soda everyone
can hear me!

Knock Knock.
Who's there?
Chooch
Chooch who?
Here comes the train!

Knock Knock.
Who's there?
Police
Police who?
Police stop telling these silly
knock knock jokes!

Knock Knock.
Who's there?
Kook
Kook who?
Who you calling a cuckoo?

Knock Knock.
Who's there?
Too short
Too short who?
Too short to ring
the doorbell!

Knock Knock.
Who's there?
Rowan
Rowan who?
Rowan a boat is hard work!

Knock Knock.
Who's there?
Europe
Europe who?
How very rude!

Knock Knock.
Who's there?
Omar
Omar who?
Omar goodness! Wrong door!

Knock Knock.
Who's there?
Amigo
Amigo who?
Amigo to bed, I'm very tired

Knock Knock.
Who's there?
Cash
Cash who?
Are you some kind of nut?

Knock Knock.
Who's there?
Alpaca
Alpaca who?
Alpaca suitcase... let's go!

Knock Knock.
Who's there?
Lemmie
Lemmie who?
Lemmie kiss you?

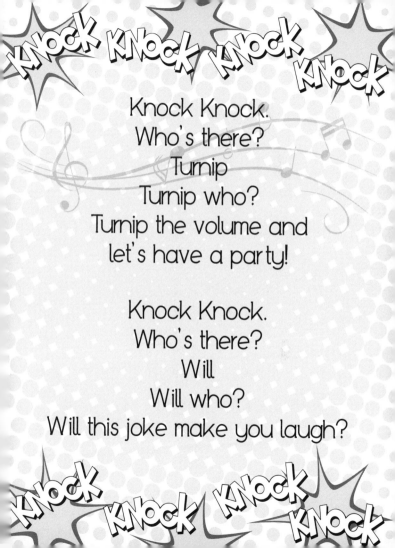

Knock Knock.
Who's there?
Turnip
Turnip who?
Turnip the volume and
let's have a party!

Knock Knock.
Who's there?
Will
Will who?
Will this joke make you laugh?

Knock Knock.
Who's there?
Harry
Harry who?
Harry up and open the door!

Knock Knock.
Who's there?
Theodore
Theodore who?
Theodore wasn't open,
so I knocked

Knock Knock.
Who's there?
Al
Al who?
Al give you a hug if
you open the door

Knock Knock.
Who's there?
Nana
Nana who?
nana your business!

KNOCK KNOCK KNOCK KNOCK

Knock Knock.
Who's there?
Wanda
Wanda who?
Did you Wanda who
was knocking?

Knock Knock.
Who's there?
Snow
Snow who?
Snow use! I forgot my name!

KNOCK KNOCK KNOCK KNOCK

Knock Knock.
Who's there?
Sherlock
Sherlock who?
Sherlock your door
tight shut!

Knock Knock.
Who's there?
Ben
Ben who?
Ben knocking for 10 minutes!

Knock Knock.
Who's there?
Robin
Robin who?
Robin you! Hand over the cash!

Knock Knock.
Who's there?
Luke
Luke who?
Luke through the
keyhole and see!

Knock Knock.
Who's there?
Needle
Needle who?
Needle little help
opening the door?

Knock Knock.
Who's there?
Noah
Noah who?
Noah what time it is?

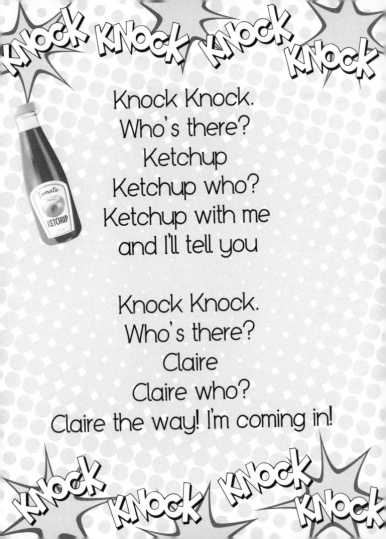

Knock Knock.
Who's there?
Ketchup
Ketchup who?
Ketchup with me
and I'll tell you

Knock Knock.
Who's there?
Claire
Claire who?
Claire the way! I'm coming in!

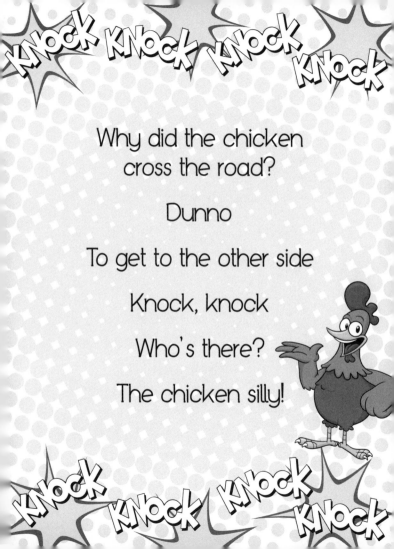

Knock Knock.
Who's there?
Icing
Icing who?
Icing so loud the
neighbours can hear me!

Knock Knock.
Who's there?
Radio
Radio who?
Radio or not... here I come!

Knock Knock.
Who's there?
Howl
Howl who?
Howl you know it's really me
unless you open the door?

Knock Knock.
Who's there?
Watson
Watson who?
Watson TV tonight?

Knock Knock.
Who's there?
Wendy
Wendy who?
Wendy bell works again, I won't
have to knock anymore!

Knock Knock.
Who's there?
Arfur
Arfur who?
Arfur got!

Knock Knock.
Who's there?
Witches
Witches who?
Witches the way to go home?

Knock Knock.
Who's there?
Althea
Althea who?
Althea later alligator!

Knock Knock.
Who's there?
Norma Lee
Norma Lee who?
Norma Lee I don't go round
knocking on doors!

Knock Knock.
Who's there?
Viper
Viper who?
Viper nose, it's running

Knock Knock.
Who's there?
Abbot
Abbot who?
Abbot you don't know
who this is?

Knock Knock.
Who's there?
Annie
Annie who?
Annie one you like!

Knock Knock.
Who's there?
King Tut
King Tut who?
King Tut key fried chicken!

Knock Knock.
Who's there?
Robin
Robin who?
Robin the piggy bank again

Knock Knock.
Who's there?
Sadie
Sadie who?
Sadie magic word!

Knock Knock.
Who's there?
Justin
Justin who?
Justin time for dinner

Knock Knock.
Who's there?
Roach
Roach who?
Roach you a letter,
didn't you get it?

Knock Knock.
Who's there?
Beats
Beats who?
Beats me!

Knock Knock.
Who's there?
Déja
Déja who?
Knock Knock

Knock Knock.
Who's there?
Leaf
Leaf who?
Leaf the house and
come out and play

Knock Knock.
Who's there?
Robert Pipplesbum
Robert Pipplesbum who?
How many Robert Pipplesbums
do you know??

Knock Knock.
Who's there?
Art
Art who?
Art who D2!

Knock Knock.
Who's there?
Hawaii
Hawaii who?
I'm fine thank you,
Hawaii you?

Knock Knock.
Who's there?
Nobel
Nobel who?
Nobel, so I knocked

Knock Knock.
Who's there?
Lion
Lion who?
Lion outside the front door.

Knock Knock.
Who's there?
Major
Major who?
Major day with this joke,
haven't I?

Knock Knock.
Who's there?
Mavis
Mavis who?
mavis be a warning to you to
watch out for silly jokes!

Knock Knock.
Who's there?
Irish
Irish who?
Irish you a nice day

Knock Knock.
Who's there?
A pile up
A pile up who?
Yuck!

Knock Knock.
Who's there?
I got up
I got up who?
You better go to
the toilet then!

KNOCK KNOCK KNOCK KNOCK

Knock Knock.
Who's there?
Icy
Icy who?
Open the door and
I can see you too

Knock Knock.
Who's there?
Wire
Wire who?
Wire you not opening the door?

KNOCK KNOCK KNOCK KNOCK

Knock Knock.
Who's there?
Bolivia
Bolivia who?
I can't Bolivia you don't
remember me!

Knock Knock.
Who's there?
Sweden
Sweden who?
Sweden sour chicken!

Knock Knock.
Who's there?
Kenya
Kenya who?
Kenya feel the love tonight?

Knock Knock.
Who's there?
Caesar
Caesar who?
Caesar quick! She's
trying to run away!

Knock Knock.
Who's there?
Armageddon
Armageddon who?
Armageddon bored of
standing outside this door!

Knock Knock.
Who's there?
Lena
Lena who?
Lena bit closer... I'll tell you!

Knock Knock.
Who's there?
Ira
Ira who?
Ira gret I don't know
any better jokes!

Knock Knock.
Who's there?
Anita
Anita who?
Anita little love
and understanding

Knock Knock.
Who's there?
Hannah
Hannah who?
Hannah n other thing!

Knock Knock.
Who's there?
Abigail
Abigail who?
Abigail came and blew
my hat off!

Knock Knock.
Who's there?
Some Bunny
Some Bunny who?
Some Bunny ate all
my carrots!

Knock Knock.
Who's there?
Broccoli
Broccoli who?
Broccoli doesn't
have a last name!

Knock Knock.
Who's there?
Looking for a lass
Looking for a lass who?
Cowboy shop is down the road

Knock Knock.
Who's there?
Claire
Claire who?
Claire off! I don't like
Knock Knock jokes!

Knock Knock.
Who's there?
Doctor
Doctor who?
Let me in the Daleks are here!

Knock Knock.
Who's there?
Arfur
Arfur who?
Arfur pound of tupenny rice

KNOCK KNOCK KNOCK KNOCK

Knock Knock.
Who's there?
Poop
Poop who?
Toilet's over there

Knock Knock.
Who's there?
Do you want 2 CDs?
Do you want 2 CDs who?
Do you want 2 CDs pictures
of me as a baby?

KNOCK KNOCK KNOCK KNOCK

Knock Knock.
Who's there?
Mister Buzz
Mister Buzz who?
Mister Buzz? Then get a taxi!

Knock Knock.
Who's there?
Twain
Twain who?
Twain wuns on a twack

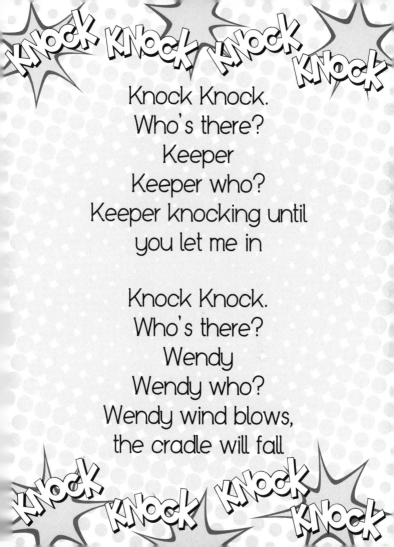

Knock Knock.
Who's there?
Keeper
Keeper who?
Keeper knocking until
you let me in

Knock Knock.
Who's there?
Wendy
Wendy who?
Wendy wind blows,
the cradle will fall

Knock Knock.
Who's there?
Cockadoodle
Cockadoodle who?
Time to get up!

Knock Knock.
Who's there?
Vindle
Vindle who?
Loo roll is in the fridge!

Knock Knock.
Who's there?
Anise
Anise who?
Anise eed balls

Knock Knock.
Who's there?
Lauren
Lauren who?
Lauren order stops criminals

Knock Knock.
Who's there?
Sheila
Sheila who?
Sheila be coming round the
mountain when she comes!

Knock Knock.
Who's there?
Polly
Polly who?
Polly put the kettle on

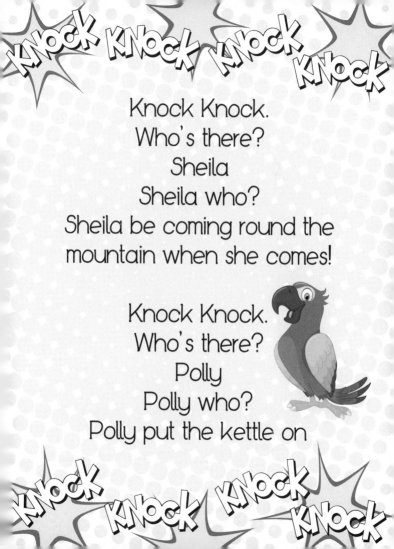

Knock Knock.
Who's there?
Ju
Ju who?
Ju want to come
round to my house?

Knock Knock.
Who's there?
Olive
Olive who?
I love you too!

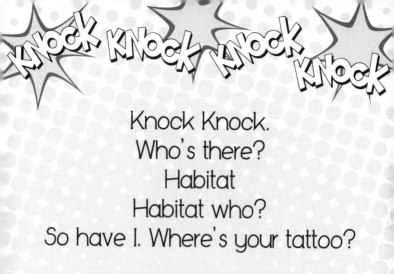

Knock Knock.
Who's there?
Habitat
Habitat who?
So have I. Where's your tattoo?

Knock Knock.
Who's there?
Yabu
Yabu who?
The jokes not that bad!

Knock Knock.
Who's there?
Whale meat
Whale meat who?
Whale meat again, don't know
where, don't know when

Knock Knock.
Who's there?
Angus
Angus who?
Angus my coat up

Knock Knock.
Who's there?
Michelle
Michelle who?
Michelle suits in the wash

Knock Knock.
Who's there?
Jen
Jen who?
Jen know what time it is?

Knock Knock.
Who's there?
Ella
Ella who?
Ella va lot of coffee in Brazil

Knock Knock.
Who's there?
Linda
Linda who?
Linda s a fiver?

Knock Knock.
Who's there?
Barbara
Barbara who?
Barbara black sheep

Knock Knock.
Who's there?
Igor
Igor who?
Igor a feeling you're not
going to open the door!

Knock Knock.
Who's there?
Toby
Toby who?
Toby or not to be,
that is the question

Knock Knock.
Who's there?
Diane
Diane who?
Diane to meet you!

Knock Knock.
Who's there?
Sharon
Sharon who?
Sharon is caring

Knock Knock.
Who's there?
Shirley
Shirley who?
Shirley some mistake?

Knock Knock.
Who's there?
Warren
Warren who?
Warren Peace

Knock Knock.
Who's there?
Willy
Willy who?
Willy ever do as he's told?

Knock Knock.
Who's there?
Watson
Watson who?
Watson a nice girl like you
doing in a place like this?

Knock Knock.
Who's there?
Donna
Donna who?
Donna kebab

Knock Knock.
Who's there?
Lucille
Lucille who?
Lucille on your shoe
will make you fall over!

Knock Knock.
Who's there?
Winston
Winston who?
Winston, you lose some

Knock Knock.
Who's there?
Olivia
Olivia who?
Olivia. Where do you live?

Knock Knock.
Who's there?
Sienna
Sienna who?
Sienna thing you like?

KNOCK KNOCK KNOCK KNOCK

Knock Knock.
Who's there?
Ewan
Ewan who?
Ewan me go out for tea?

Knock Knock.
Who's there?
Isadora
Isadora who?
Isadora door.
Even when it's a jar?

KNOCK KNOCK KNOCK KNOCK

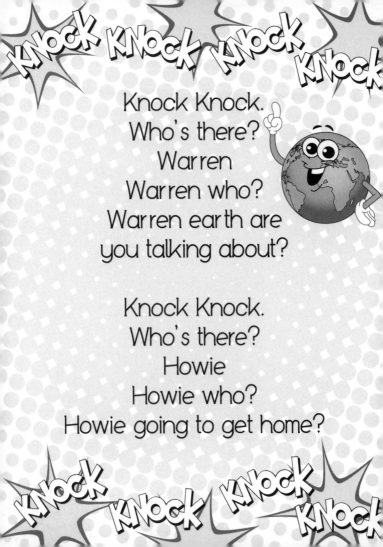

Knock Knock.
Who's there?
Jonas
Jonas who?
Jonus for dinner?

Knock Knock.
Who's there?
Gail
Gail who?
Gail force winds are forecast

Knock Knock.
Who's there?
Delia
Delia who?
Delia cards and let's
get on with the game!

Knock Knock.
Who's there?
Goat
Goat who?
Goat who Bed!

Knock Knock.
Who's there?
Jamaica
Jamaica who?
No, she did it herself!

Knock Knock.
Who's there?
Zulus
Zulus who?
No, I won!

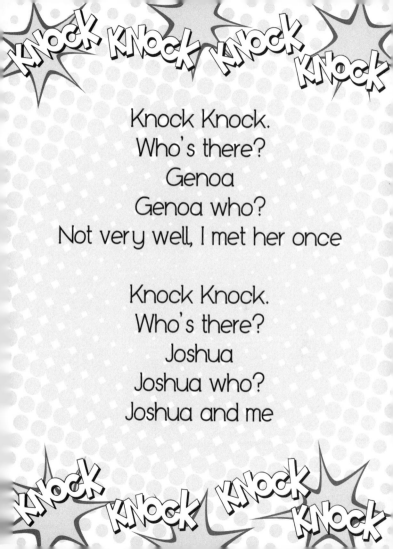

Knock Knock.
Who's there?
Genoa
Genoa who?
Not very well, I met her once

Knock Knock.
Who's there?
Joshua
Joshua who?
Joshua and me

Knock Knock.
Who's there?
Letitia
Letitia who?
You've got a bad cold!

Knock Knock.
Who's there?
Lynette
Lynette who?
Lynette all the cakes!

Knock Knock.
Who's there?
Tamara
Tamara who?
Tamara never comes

Knock Knock.
Who's there?
Sonya
Sonya who?
Sonya coat, I think
it's bird poo!

Knock Knock.
Who's there?
Marian
Marian who?
Marian acrobat.
They will bend over
backwards to make
you happy!

Knock Knock.
Who's there?
Nanette
Nanette who?
Nanette Grandad's dinner!

Knock Knock.
Who's there?
Done Up
Done Up who?
I hope you wiped your bum!

Knock Knock.
Who's there?
Ulrika
Ulrika who?
Ulrika poo if I stand in some!

Knock Knock.
Who's there?
Miss Yen
Miss Yen who?
Miss Yen impossible!

Knock Knock.
Who's there?
Homer
Homer who?
Homer lone

Knock Knock.
Who's there?
Abby
Abby who?
Abby seeing you later!

KNOCK KNOCK KNOCK KNOCK

Knock Knock.
Who's there?
Norbert
Norbert who?
Norbert the best
for you, my dear!

Knock Knock.
Who's there?
Anatolia
Anatolia who?
Anatolia once! I'm not
telling you again!

KNOCK KNOCK KNOCK KNOCK

Knock Knock.
Who's there?
Anita
Anita who?
Anita borrow a pencil

Knock Knock.
Who's there?
Yukon
Yukon who?
Yukon say that again!

Knock Knock.
Who's there?
Abe
Abe who?
Abe C D E F G H...

Knock Knock.
Who's there?
Ada
Ada who?
Ada burger for my lunch

Knock Knock.
Who's there?
Amy
Amy who?
Amy fraid I've forgotten!

Knock Knock.
Who's there?
Alma
Alma who?
Alma not going to tell you!

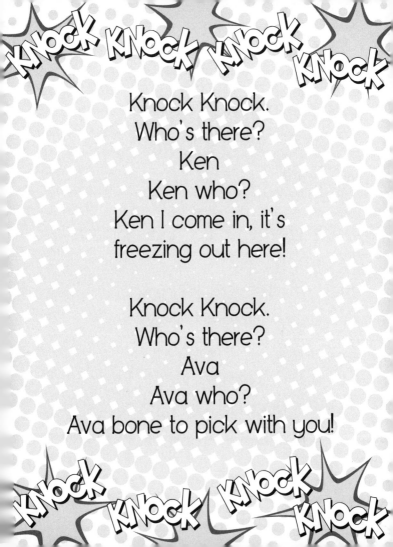

Knock Knock.
Who's there?
Will
Will who?
Will you listen to another Knock Knock joke?

Knock Knock.
Who's there?
Eddy
Eddy who?
Eddy body home?

Knock Knock.
Who's there?
Erin
Erin who?
I have a quick Erin to run,
but I'll be back!

Knock Knock.
Who's there?
Ben
Ben who?
Ben away for a while,
but I'm back now!